Everyday Maths

Second edition

D1340834

Brown and Brown

Publishers: Brown and Brown,
                Keeper's Cottage,
                Westward,
                Wigton
                Cumbria CA7 8NQ
                Tel. 016973 42915

First published 1992
Reprinted 1994 & 1997

Second edition 2000
Reprinted 2001 & 2003

ISBN 1 870596 73 0

Printed by Reed's Ltd., Penrith, Cumbria on 100% recycled paper and card.

Introduction

This book of exercises provides practice in the basic maths needed by adults in everyday life. Mathematics in real situations is often not a precise skill. Because of this, many of the exercises include an element of estimation or require interpretation of the facts given. Some questions test the reader's practical knowledge of common sizes, quantities and costs. A calculator is essential for only a few of the exercises, otherwise readers may choose whether or not to use one.

The exercises are in random order so that items of interest can be selected as preferred. The index (p.48) is a guide to the mathematical topics and skills covered. Detailed answers are given (pp.42-47), although some are open to discussion or individual interpretation. Prices are correct at the time of publication but will, inevitably, go out of date.

Second edition

The text for this **Second edition** has been extensively revised and re-written. The questions have been altered to take into account the changes in Weights & Measures legislation from 1st January 2000 and all prices and examples have been updated where necessary.

For a current catalogue of publications, please contact:

Brown and Brown, Keeper's Cottage, Westward, Wigton, Cumbria CA7 8NQ   *Tel. 016973 42915*

Contents

Fruit and Vegetables

1. *In the market there are 2 1/2 kg bags of potatoes for 78p and loose potatoes at 25p per kg.*
   Which is cheaper ?

2. *Whole cucumbers cost 72p. Half cucumbers cost 42p.*
   Which is the better buy ?

3. How many medium size apples would you expect to get if you asked for 1/2 kg of apples ?

4. *Large oranges are 28p each or 4 for £1.10.*
   How much will you save if you buy 4 ?

BANANAS
£1.06
per kilo

APPLES
£1.36
per kilo

PEARS
£1.28
per kilo

5. *You have bought some fruit on a market stall and you think that the man may have charged you too much.*

You bought:

> $^1/_2$ *kg bananas @ £1.06 per kilo*
>
> *1 kg apples @ £1.36 per kilo*
>
> $^3/_4$ *kg pears @ £1.28 per kilo*

a. *He charged you £2.85.*
Did he charge you too much ?

b. *He gave you £6.15 change from a £10 note.*
Did he short change you ?

Maths about the house - 1

1. Light bulbs

Standard light bulbs are:

40 watt   60 watt   75 watt   100 watt   150 watt

a. Which will give the brightest light ?

b. Which would you choose for a table lamp ?

c. Which would you choose for the main room light ?

d. What do you think it would cost to leave a 150 watt bulb on for 12 hours ?

   3p   12p   25p

e. *A low energy bulb can cost as much as £10 to buy but, because it uses a lot less electricity and lasts 10 times as long, it will save you money.*

   How much do you think it could save in the long run ?

   £7   £29   £46

2. Telephones

a. Which number do you dial for the Fire Brigade in an emergency ?

b. Which number do you dial for the Coastguard in an emergency ?

c. Which *BT* number do you dial for the Operator ?

d. Which *BT* number do you dial for Directory Enquiries ?

e. Which *BT* number do you dial to find out the number of the last person who called you ?

3. Laundry

Clothes are marked with temperature symbols to show how they should be washed. The symbols are:

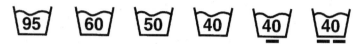

a. Which is the hottest ?

b. What do the numbers **95, 60, 50** and **40** mean ?

c. What is the temperature of boiling water ?

d. What sort of material is this symbol used for ? $\boxed{95}$

e. What sort of material is this symbol used for ? $\boxed{40}$

4. Paint

Most paint comes in tins of these sizes:

1l   250ml   5l   2.5l   500ml

a. Which is the smallest size ?

b. If you wanted enough emulsion paint for the walls in a couple of rooms, which size would you buy ?

c. If you wanted some gloss paint for 2 doors, which size would you buy ?

d. If you wanted some varnish for a coffee table top, which size would you buy ?

Dates and Calendars

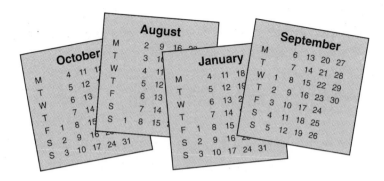

1. It is Monday, February 8th and you have to make an appointment for Friday. What date will it be ?

2. It is Thursday, April 22nd when someone tells you that they will visit you next Tuesday. What date will it be ?

3. What date will it be one week after Saturday, November 27th ?

4. On Thursday, 29th July someone says they will meet you in a fortnight's time. What date will it be ?

5. It is Wednesday, December 15th. You have to fill in a report form about an accident you had last Friday. What was the date ?

6. It is Sunday, 16th May and your mother's birthday is on 25th May. What day of the week will it be ?

7. Yesterday's paper is dated June 29th. What date will it be the day after tomorrow ?

8. Good Friday falls on March 29th. What date will Easter Monday be ?

Migraine Tablets

This pack contains Migraleve Pink and Migraleve Yellow tablets.
Always start with Migraleve Pink tablets.
- Migraleve Pink tablets have a unique double action providing powerful relief from migraine headache and associated nausea and vomiting. If taken at the first sign of a migraine, Migraleve Pink tablets can prevent an attack from developing.
- Migraleve Yellow tablets provide relief for continuing migraine symptoms. They should always be taken <u>after</u> the first dose of Migraleve Pink tablets.

Dose for adults:
- 2 Migraleve Pink tablets to be swallowed at the first sign of a migraine attack.
- If the migraine persists, then take 2 Migraleve Yellow tablets every 4 hours after the Migraleve Pink dose.
- Do not take more than 8 tablets (2 pink and 6 yellow) in a 24-hour period.

Dose for children 10-14 years of age:
- 1 Migraleve Pink tablet to be swallowed at the first sign of a migraine attack.
- If the migraine persists, then take 1 Migraleve Yellow tablet every 4 hours after the Migraleve Pink dose.
- Do not take more than 4 tablets (1 pink and 3 yellow) in a 24-hour period.

Do not give to children under 10 years of age except under medical supervision.

TRUE / FALSE

Adults

1. 2 Pink tablets can be taken every 4 hours.

2. 2 Yellow and 2 Pink tablets can be taken in the first 4 hours.

3. 2 Yellow tablets can be taken every 4 hours throughout the day.

4. Pink tablets should always be taken first.

5. You must not drive after taking tablets.

6. You should not drink alcohol after taking tablets.

Children

1. A child of 15 can take the adult dose.

2. A child of 12 can take 1 Pink and up to 3 Yellow tablets in 24 hours.

3. Children should start with a Yellow tablet.

4. Children under 10 should not take yellow tablets.

Olympic High Jump

The graph below shows the winning jumps, in metres, in the Olympic High Jump Competition for both men and women.

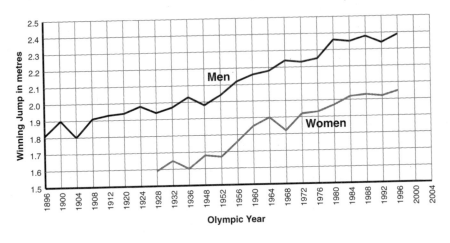

1. *The 1996 Olympic Record high jump for men was 2.39 metres.*

   a. Is 2.39 metres higher or lower than the top of a door frame ?

   b. Is 2.39 metres higher or lower than the ceiling in a typical modern home ?

2. In which year did women first compete in the Olympic High Jump ?

3. a. In which Olympic Games did men first jump 2.0 metres ?

   b. In which Olympic Games did women first jump 2.0 metres ?

4. a. When was the last time that a man won an Olympic Gold Medal with a jump which was lower than the winning jump in the previous games ?

b. When was the last time that a woman won an Olympic Gold Medal with a jump which was lower than the winning jump in the previous games ?

5. *The 1996 Olympic Women's High Jump Champion was Stefka Kostadinova of Bulgaria with a jump of 2.05 metres.*

In which Olympic Games would this jump have beaten all the men's jumps ?

6. What was the difference between the winning men's and women's jumps in 1964 ?

7. Guess the 2000 Olympic men's and women's winning jumps. Compare your guess to the result and fill in the figures on the graph.

Dick Fosbury, inventor of the 'Fosbury Flop', winning the 1968 men's Olympic High Jump

Patio

You are asked to help plan and lay a patio for a friend.

The area which is to be paved measures 4.5 metres by 2.7 metres.

The paving slabs measure 450mm x 450mm.

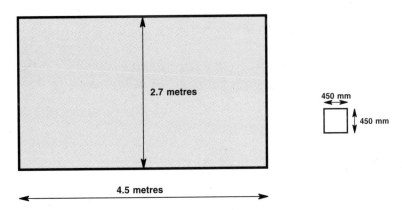

1. How many paving slabs will be needed for the patio ?

2. *The paving slabs are supplied in packs of 15 slabs.*
   How many packs will you need ?

3. *The slabs cost £2.75 each.*
   How much will it cost for all the slabs needed ?

4. *A builder is selling some second-hand slabs which measure 18 inches by 18 inches.*

   a. How many of these would be needed for the patio ?
      (**Note:** *1 metre = 39.4"*)

   b. If the second-hand slabs cost £1.05 each, how much would the patio cost ?

   c. How much would you save by using the second-hand slabs ?

Pub prices

Lager	Bitter	Whisky	Orange Juice	Wine
£2.10	£1.90	£1.20	80p	£1.80
pint	*pint*	*glass*	*glass*	*glass*

You are going to a pub with three friends.

1. If each person buys a round of drinks, how much money do you think you will need to take with you for an evening at the pub ?

2. How much will it cost for 4 half-pints of lager ?

3. How much will it cost for 4 pints of bitter ?

4. How much will it cost for a whisky, a glass of wine, a half of bitter and a pint of lager ?

5. **a.** How much will it cost for a pint of bitter, a half of lager, a whisky and orange, and a glass of wine ?

   b. What change will you get if you pay for the drinks with a £10 note ?

6. *All 4 people are drinking pints of lager and it is your round. You only have £8 left.*

   a. Can you buy everyone a pint ?

   b. What can you buy without borrowing any money from your friends ?

Shopping sizes

Eggs

a. What is the minimum number of eggs that you can usually buy in a box ?

b. How are eggs usually priced ?

c. *Eggs are graded from 1 to 7.*
Which is the largest size ?

Coffee

a. What is the smallest jar of instant coffee you can usually buy ?

50g   100g   200g

b. What would you expect (roughly) to pay for a 100g jar of coffee ?

50p   99p   £1.59   £2.92

Butter

Many people still think of butter as being sold by the half pound.
What is the actual metric weight that you get when you buy a 'half pound' pack ?

100g   250g   500g

Cheese

Cheese is now sold by the kilogram. (Before January 1st 2000, it was sold by the pound.)
If the cost of mature Scottish Cheddar is £6.59 per kilo, how much will 250g cost ?

Crisps

Potatoes can be bought for about 25p per kg. Crisps are just thin slices of potato, fried and flavoured.

If a bag of crisps costs about 27p and weighs 25g, how much would a kilogram of crisps cost ?

Fruit Juice

'Long-life' fruit juices, such as apple juice and orange juice, are commonly sold in cartons.

What is the volume of a standard-size carton ?

250ml   1 pint   1 litre

Bread

Roughly how many slices of bread do you think there are in an average medium-sliced loaf ?

17   22   27   32

Sardines

A tin of sardines contains about 120g of fish and costs about 37p.
How much would a kilogram of tinned sardines cost ?

Wine

What is the volume of a standard wine bottle ?

50cl   75cl   1 pint   1 litre

Making custard

DIRECTIONS

1. Put 2 tablespoons of custard powder into a basin with 1-2 tablespoons of sugar.
2. Mix to a paste with milk taken from 1 pint (568ml).
3. Heat remainder of milk to nearly boiling point and pour on to the mixed custard stirring well.
4. Return the custard to the saucepan and bring to the boil, stirring all the time. MAKES 5 SERVINGS

MICROWAVE METHOD (700W OVEN)

1. Follow points 1 and 2 for the standard make up.
2. Add remaining milk and cook on FULL power for 6 minutes (increase cooking time for a lower wattage oven).
3. Stir halfway through cooking.

1. How much sugar would you put in for 5 people ?

2. Do you need to boil the milk ?

3. Do you add the mixed paste to the hot milk ?

4. For how many minutes should you set a 700W microwave oven ?

5. How long would you need to cook the custard in a 600W microwave oven ?

6. Would it be quicker to make custard in a microwave ?

7. Would making custard in a microwave save any washing up ?

8. If you were making custard for 2 people, what quantities would you use ?

Distances

1. How far is a mile ? Can you name a building or a place which is 1 mile from your home ?

2. How many minutes would it take you to walk a mile ?

3. How fast do you walk, in miles per hour ?

4. If a car travels at a mile a minute, how fast is it going in m.p.h. ? How fast is that in kilometres per hour ?

5. How many miles (if any) are you from your home at the moment ?

6. How far is it to your nearest Post Office ?

7. How far is it to your nearest 'phone box ?

8. How far is it to the place where you were born ?

9. How far is it from your home to London ? *

10. How far is it from your home to Inverness ? *

11. How far is it from your home to Cardiff ? *

12. How far is it from your home to Belfast ? *

* *If you live in London, Inverness, Cardiff or Belfast, give the distance from your home to a landmark in the centre of your city.*

Wallpaper

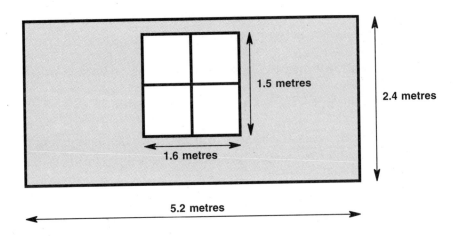

1. What is the area of the wall, including the window, in square metres ?

2. What is the area of the window ?

3. What is the area of the wall, excluding the window ?

4. *Rolls of wallpaper are often 10m x 52cm.*
   What area will one roll cover ?

5. How many rolls of wallpaper will be needed for the wall shown above ?

6. If the wallpaper costs £6.49 per roll, what will it cost to wallpaper the wall ?

Wallpaper paste

Application per sachet	Quantity of Cold Water	Approx. Coverage
Normal wallpapers, including woodchip	12 pints	8-10 rolls
Washable papers and vinyls	10 pints	8 rolls
Blown vinyls (*e.g.* Permabos, Fresco)	10 pints	8 rolls
Novamura	8 pints	6 rolls
Embossed papers (*e.g.* Anaglypta Original)	8 pints	4-5 rolls
Heavy embossed papers (*e.g.* Anaglypta SupaDurable)	7 pints	3-4 rolls
Polystyrene tiles	7 pints	160 sq. ft.

MIXING Sprinkle contents into water, stirring briskly for 30 seconds. Leave for 3 minutes, then stir well before pasting.

1. What is the maximum number of rolls of wallpaper that this sachet will cover ?

2. How many rolls of embossed paper will the sachet cover ?

3. How many pints of water are needed for mixing the paste for use with embossed paper ?

4. How many gallons of water are needed for mixing the paste for use with Novamura paper ?

5. Should you empty the contents into a bucket and then add the water ?

6. Do you wait 3 minutes before stirring the contents ?

7. What area of polystyrene tiles will the sachet fix ?

8. How many 6″ x 6″ tiles will the sachet fix ?

TV Guide

6.00 REGIONAL NEWS MAGAZINE

6.30 **ITV EVENING NEWS:** Weather & Regional Weather

7.00 EMMERDALE

7.30 HIGH ROAD

8.00 **THE BILL: Crash Landing**. A small plane lands in Sun Hill.

9.00 **PEAK PRACTICE: Change of Life.** Another episode about the Peak District doctors.

10.00 **THE BIG MATCH:** Champions' League Highlights.

11.00 **ITV NIGHTLY NEWS:** Weather

11.20 **REGIONAL NEWS:** Weather

11.30 **ANATOMY OF A DISASTER:** Footage of volcanoes erupting as seen from helicopters.

12.35 **YOUNG, GIFTED AND BROKE:** Showcase for performers.

1.05 **THE BIG MATCH:** The whole of one of tonight's European Champions' League matches.

2.40 **SINGAPORE SLING:** Feature length Australian drama about a private detective living in Singapore.

4.10 BEST OF BRITISH MOTORSPORT

4.40 **ITV NIGHTSCREEN:** Text-based information.

1. How long does *High Road* last ?

   a. in minutes   **b.** in hours

2. How long is there between the end of *Emmerdale* and the start of *Peak Practice* ?

3. How long does *ITV Nightly News & Weather* last, in minutes?

4. How long does the later *Big Match* last, in minutes ?

5. What time does *The Bill* start ? What time is that on the 24-hour clock ?

6. What time does *Best of British Motorsport* start ? What time is that on the 24-hour clock ?

7. What are the starting and finishing times of *ITV Evening News, Weather & Regional Weather* on the 24-hour clock ?

8. If you started a 180-minute video tape with *Young, Gifted and Broke*, would you get all of *Singapore Sling* on it as well ?

9. Could you record all the sports programmes on a 180-minute video tape ?

10. What *on* and *off* time settings would you need for the video to record these programmes?

    a. *Regional News Magazine*

    b. *Peak Practice*

    c. *Anatomy of a Disaster*

Fractions, decimals & percentages

A.

	1 Fraction	2 Decimal	3 Percentage	4 Proportion
Half				
Third				
Quarter				
Fifth				
Eighth				
Tenth				

1. Fill in the fraction which is the same as the word in the left-hand column.

   $1/8$ $1/5$ $1/2$ $1/10$ $1/4$ $1/3$

2. Fill in the decimal which is about the same as the word in the left-hand column.

   0.1   0.25   0.125   0.5   0.33   0.2

3. Fill in the percentage which is about the same as the word in the left-hand column

25%   20%   50%   10%   12.5%   33.3%

4. Fill in the proportion which is the same as the word in the left-hand column.

1 in 3   1 in 2   1 in 10   1 in 8   1 in 5   1 in 4

B. Write the fraction and percentage which are the same as the black portion in each of these diagrams:

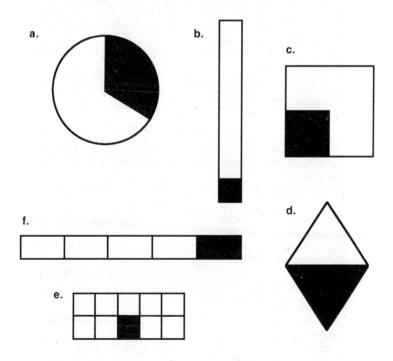

a.

b.

c.

f.

e.

d.

McDonald's

EXTRA VALUE MEALS

medium meals served with medium fries and medium soft drink
large meals served with large fries and large soft drink

	MEDIUM £2.99	LARGE £3.19

1 **BIG MAC™ MEAL**
2 **McCHICKEN™ SANDWICH MEAL**
3 **QUARTER POUNDER' with Cheese MEAL**
4 **VEGETABLE DELUXE MEAL**
5 **CHICKEN McNUGGETS™ MEAL** (6 Pieces)
6 **FILET O' FISH™ MEAL**

† 113.4 grams pre-cooked weight

CHILDREN'S HAPPY MEALS™ £1.99

served with regular fries, regular soft drink and a toy

HAMBURGER HAPPY MEAL™
CHEESEBURGER HAPPY MEAL™'
CHICKEN McNUGGETS HAPPY MEAL™ (4 Pieces)
FISH FINGERS HAPPY MEAL™ (3 Pieces)

DESSERTS

SUNDAES (Hot Fudge, Hot Caramel, Strawberry) £0.89
HOT APPLE PIE £0.70 with ICE CREAM £0.99
DONUTS (Chocolate, Cinnamon, Sugar flavours) £0.59
TAKE AWAY PRICE* £0.50
ICE CREAM CONE £0.35 with *99 flake* £0.45

SANDWICHES

BIG MAC™ £1.90
McCHICKEN™ SANDWICH £1.90
QUARTER POUNDER' with Cheese £1.90
VEGETABLE DELUXE £1.59
FILET O'FISH™ (100% Pure Cod) £1.59
CHICKEN McNUGGETS™
  6 Pieces £1.59   9 Pieces £2.21   20 Pieces £4.53
HAMBURGER £0.69   **CHEESEBURGER** £0.79

† 113.4 grams pre-cooked weight

FRENCH FRIES

REGULAR £0.59   MEDIUM £0.89   LARGE £0.99

1. Why do McDonald's call their chips *French Fries*, and why do they have *Large, Medium,* and *Regular* portions, not *Large, Medium* and *Small* ?

2. What is the difference between the cost of a *Big Mac* and a *Vegetable DeLuxe*.

3. a. How much does it cost for a hamburger and a large portion of chips ?

    b. What change would you get from £2 ?

4. a. How much is it for a *McChicken Sandwich* and *Medium Fries* ?

    b. What change would you get from £10 ?

5. a. How much would it cost to take away 2 *Donuts* and an *Ice Cream Cone with 99 Flake* ?

    b. What change would you get from £5 ?

6. a. How much does it cost for a *Filet O'Fish* meal, a medium portion of chips and a medium soft drink ?

    b. What change would you get from £20 ?

7. Use a calculator to work out the exact price of each *Chicken McNugget* if you buy 6, 9 or 20.

8. You don't want to spend more than £8 on lunch for yourself and 2 children. Work out a possible lunch you could have.

Cars for Sale

a. **ESCORT** 5-door hatchback, 1992 (J), 44,580 miles, red, MoT, taxed, vgc **£1595** Tel. 01254 885998

b. **FIESTA 1.1LX** M reg. 66,000 genuine miles, red, 5-door, radio cassette, 5 spd, MoT Aug. 2000, taxed. Superb. **£2,995 OVNO. PX considered.** Tel. 0161 652 4394

c. **FORD FIESTA 1.1 LI** K reg. only 46,000 mls, 5-door, immobiliser, alarm, sunroof. **£1,995** Tel. 01942 601171

d. **FORD ESCORT 1.8SI** R reg. 11k miles April 1998, FSH, CD player, 1 careful owner from new. **£7,300** Tel. 01244 547446

e. **FORD ESCORT ECLIPSE LTD. ED. 1.3** H reg. met. red, remote alarm, superb condition. **£1,295 INC. WARRANTY** Tel. 0161 480 1312

f. **FORD ESCORT COSWORTH LOOKALIKE** 1.3 engine, K reg. 55K miles, leather interior, alloys, spoiler. 1 owner **£2,395** Tel. 0161 474 0011

g. **FORD ESCORT 1.8 TURBO DIESEL** 1996, N reg. 90k miles, 4-dr saloon, new shape, 12 months MoT, PAS, rad/cass. ex. cond. **£3,495** Tel. 01772 628644

h. **FORD FOCUS 1.8 ZETEC** 1999 3-door, black, 10,000 miles, Sony CD system, climate pack, company car forces sale. **£11,000 OVNO.** Tel. 01928 725300

i. **FORD GRANADA 2.0 GLI** G reg. magenta red, boot spoiler, PAS, ABS, EW, CL, towing bar, taxed, MoT, very reliable. **£1,290 ONO** Tel. 01228 599989

j. **FORD KA** 1997 P reg. 13,000 miles, 1300cc, 3-door saloon finished in purple. **£4,999** Tel. 01257 230300

k. **FORD KA** bright red, lady owner, low miles, FSH, as new **£4,500** Tel. 01565 631476

l. **FORD MONDEO 1.8 GLX 16V** 1993 K reg. 5-door hatchback, metallic grey, e/windows, c/locking, e/mirrors, average miles, genuine trade bargain. **£1,995 NO PX, NO OFFERS** Tel. 01282 425367

m. **FORD MONDEO 1.6L** 1994 L reg. very clean car, airbag, PAS, stereo, excellent runner, high miles hence very cheap car. **£1,750 ONO** Tel. 01606 883179

n. **FORD MONDEO 2.0 GLX** N reg. low miles, 5-door hatch, metallic plum, full dealer history, elec. windows & mirrors, alarm, ABS, beautiful condition inside & out. **£4,799 ONO** Tel. 01706 812880

o. **FORD MONDEO 1.8 LX TD ESTATE** 1995 M reg. aubergine, 74k miles, taxed, MoT, good condition. **£4,500** Tel. 01925 633921

p. **FORD ORION 1.8I GHIA SI** K reg. red, electric windows, mirror & sunroof, alloy wheels, CD stereo, alarm, immobiliser, lowered suspension, stunning looks & performance, long MoT & tax. **£2,695 INC. WARRANTY** Tel. 0161 612 8549

1. How many Ford cars are there for sale ?

2. There are 4 *Ford Mondeos* advertised. Which is the newest ?

3. If you wanted a fast car and you didn't want to spend much more than £2,500, which cars would you consider ?

4. Car *n.* is advertised at £4,799 ONO. What would be your first offer for it if you thought it was a good buy ?

5. A car which is advertised as *P reg.* would have been registered in which year ?

6. What change was made to yearly car registration letters in 1999 ?

7. Which has the bigger engine ?
   a. *Ford Escort 1.3*
   b. *Ford Ka 1300cc*

8. a. Which is the cheapest car advertised ?
   b. Which is the most expensive car advertised ?

9. Which car would you expect to give the best m.p.g. ?

10. What do these abbreviations mean ?

FSH	MoT	PX	PAS
ABS	EW	CL	90K

Maths about the house - 2

1. Plugs and Fuses

Fuses in electric plugs can be:

3 amp   5 amp   13 amp

a. Which fuse would be needed for something which uses a lot of electricity, like an electric kettle ?

b. Would a table lamp need a large or a small fuse ?

c. Which electrical item uses so much electricity that it needs a special circuit for itself ?

Refrigerator   Tumble Drier   Electric Cooker

Immersion Heater in a Hot Water Tank

2. Ironing

Clothes are marked with symbols to show how they should be ironed:

a. Which is the coolest setting ?

b. Should polyester be ironed on a hotter or cooler setting than wool ?

c. Which setting should you use for ironing pure wool ?

d. Which symbol tells you not to iron ?

3. Cooking maths

a. Which is the largest size spoon ?

teaspoon   tablespoon   dessertspoon

b. Which is the larger - a pint or a litre ?

c. Which is the larger - a gram or an ounce ?

d. Which is the larger - a pound or a kilogram ?

e. Which is the hottest - *200°C; 200°F; Gas Mark 8* ?

4. Paper

The International sizes of paper are:

A1   A2   A3   A4   A5   A6

a. Which is the largest size ?

b. Which is the standard size of paper used in a ring binder and for most official letters and forms ?

c. What, would you guess, are the measurements of the standard paper size ?

i. About 200m x 300mm   ii. About 8" x 12"

iii. About 250mm x 500mm   iv. About 6" x 9"

d. What size of paper is half the standard size (*i.e. the same size as one page in this book*) ?

e. What size of envelope takes an A5 sheet unfolded ?

C4   C5   C6

Fridge Freezers

Save £15

Candy CP3012 (*Our normal price* £334.99)	NOW **£319.99**	SAVE **£15**
Hotpoint RF64 (*Our normal price* £404.99)	NOW **£379.99**	SAVE **£25**
Siemens KG-28V20 (*Our normal price* £389.99)	NOW **£349.99**	SAVE **£40**
Whirlpool ART 826 (*Our normal price* £399.99)	NOW **£379.99**	SAVE **£20**
Zanussi ZK60/30 (*Our normal price* £429.99)	NOW **£399.99**	SAVE **£30**

1. Which fridge freezer is the cheapest ?

2. Which fridge freezer is the most expensive ?

3. What is the difference between the normal full price of the *Candy* and that of the *Hotpoint* ?

4. What is the difference between the sale price of the *Siemens* and that of the *Zanussi* ?

5. Which fridge freezer seems to be the best bargain ?

6. Why do you think the amount saved varies from model to model ?

7. a. The *Zanussi* costs £21 a year to run. How much would it cost to run for 10 years ?

   b. The *Whirlpool* costs £39 a year to run. How much would it cost to run for 10 years ?

   c. What is the total cost of the *Zanussi* after 10 years, including buying it and the running cost ?

   d. What is the total cost of the *Whirlpool* after 10 years ?

   e. Which is cheaper after 10 years - the *Zanussi* or the *Whirlpool* ? What is the difference in cost ?

What size are you ?

Fill in the sizes *(imperial and metric)* for yourself and someone else *(**e.g.** partner, friend or member of family).*

MAN

Height: Weight:

	Imperial	Metric
Neck		
Chest		
Waist		
Inside leg		
Shoe size		

WOMAN

Height: Weight:

General clothes size:

	Imperial	Metric
Bust		
Waist		
Hips		
Skirt length		
Shoe size		

World population

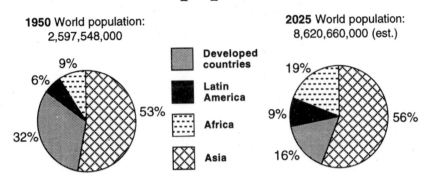

1950 World population:
2,597,548,000

2025 World population:
8,620,660,000 (est.)

Developed countries

Latin America

Africa

Asia

1. In 1950:

a.   Which area had 9% of the world's population ?

b.   Which area had just over half the world's population ?

c.   Which area had about a third of the world's population ?

d.   Which area had the smallest population ?

e.   What was the world's population in 1950, to the nearest half billion ?

2. By 2025:

a.   What is the estimated world population for the year 2025, to the nearest half billion ?

b.   What is the difference between the world's population in 2025 and that of 1950, in billions ?

c.   Which area will still have over half the world's population ?

d.   How will Africa's share of the world population have changed from 1950 to 2025 ?

e.   How will the Developed Countries' share of the world population have changed from 1950 to 2025 ?

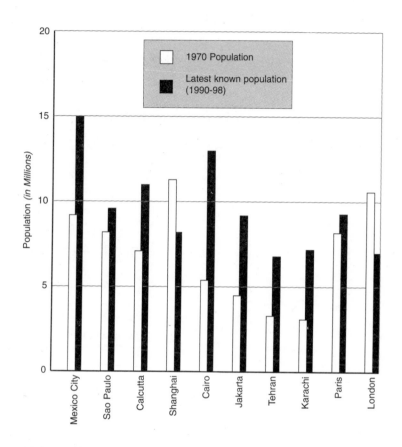

3. Cities of the world

a. Which city had a population of nearly 12 million in 1970 ?

b. Which city was the second largest in 1970 ?

c. Which cities have more than doubled in size since 1970 ?

d. Which city is now the largest of the 10 cities shown in the chart ?

e. Which 2 cities have reduced in size since 1970 ?

Travel in the U.K.

These are the some of the prices you could pay for a return journey between Edinburgh and London:

G.N.E.R.
Apex rail fare
£47

British Airways
Full price
£286

Car
(petrol only)
£67

National Express
(Coach)
Advanced Return
£25

Virgin Trains
1st Class
£225

Scottish Citylink
(Coach)
£32

British Airways
World Offer Fare
£68.70

GO
Return Air Fare
£60

1. Which is the cheapest way to travel between Edinburgh and London ?

2. Which is the most expensive way to travel ?

3. What is the difference in cost between the most expensive and the cheapest way of travelling ?

4. What is the difference in cost between the most expensive rail fare and the cheapest rail fare ?

5. Which way would you choose to travel if you wanted to arrive relaxed and not tired ?

6. Which do you think would be the fastest way to travel from Edinburgh Castle to London's Oxford Circus ?

7. Which do you think would be the slowest way to travel from Edinburgh Castle to London's Oxford Circus ?

8. If 4 people were travelling together to London and back, which means of transport would be the cheapest ?

9. Which is the most dangerous way to travel ?

10. *The price of £67 for car travel covers only the cost of petrol used by a small family car. The actual running cost of a 2-year-old car is around 35p per mile if tax, insurance, repair costs and depreciation are included.*

    If the return journey from Edinburgh to London is 760 miles, what is the overall cost ?

Gas Bill

Your gas statement

British Gas
Home Energy

Bill date & tax point	14 July 1999	
Volume conversion factor	1.022640	
Calorific value	39.9 MJ/m³	
Present reading	**03320** (E) estimated on 14 July 1999	
Previous reading	**02814** taken on 16 April 1999	
Gas used	506.0 cubic metres	
This is equivalent to	5735 kilowatt hours (kWh)	
	at 1.295 pence per kWh	
	Cost of gas used	£74.27
Standing charge	16 April 1999 to 14 July 1999	
	89 days at 7.00 pence per day	£6.23
	Sub total excluding VAT	£80.50
	VAT at 5.0%	£4.02
	Total charges	**£84.52**

1. The present reading is estimated to be 03320. This is more than the customer's reading on the meter when the bill arrived. If the customer's reading is 03217, what is the true amount of gas supplied ?

2. The charge for 506 cubic metres is £74.27. Use a calculator to work out how much it would be for the true amount of gas supplied (*i.e. the answer to Question 1*).

3. What would the new total charge be, including the standing charge ?

4. What is the difference between this total charge and the estimated bill of £84.52 ? Would you pay the estimated bill or would you ask for a new bill based on the true reading ?

Wood Filler Instructions

Mixing: Mix the filler from the tin with the catalyst paste from the tube in the following proportions:

1¹/₂" / 4 cm strip of catalyst paste to a golf ball volume of filler.

Mix thoroughly with a knife until no streaks remain and colour is uniform.

Application: Apply immediately to the area to be repaired. At normal temperatures the mix will have a working time of about 10 minutes. After 20 minutes the mix will be hard enough to carve and shape with a craft knife. After 30 minutes it is hard enough to be planed or sand-papered.

1. How long is 1¹/₂" or 4 cm ?

    a. ——————   b. ——————————

                c. ————————————————

2. How large is a golf ball ?

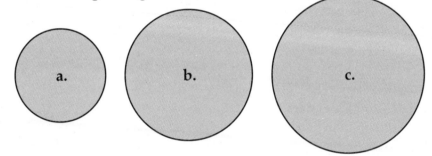

3. **True or False ?**

    a. The filler can be worked for 20 minutes.

    b. The filler can be planed after 30 minutes.

    c. The filler can be shaped with a knife after 25 minutes.

    d. The filler will remain workable longer in cold weather.

Answers

Fruit and Vegetables *(p.6/7)*

1. Loose potatoes - 62.5p for 2 1/2 kg.
2. Whole cucumbers (if you need that much!)
3. About 4.
4. 2p
5. **a.** No - he charged the correct amount.
   b. He short-changed you by £1.

Maths about the house - 1 *(p.8/9)*

1. **Light bulbs: a.** 150 watt   **b.** 60 or 75 watt (probably)
   c. 100 or 150 watt   **d.** 12p   **e.** Around £46 over 10,000 hrs. - the expected life of a low energy bulb.
2. **Telephones: a.** 999   **b.** 999   **c.** 100   **d.** 192   **e.** 1471
3. **Laundry**
   a.
   b. Temperature in °C (Celsius or Centigrade)
   c. 100°C (In Fahrenheit it is 212°F)
   d. White cotton & linen (without special finishes)
   e. Machine washable wool & wool mixes
4. **Paint: a.** 250ml   **b.** 5l   **c.** 500ml will be enough for a single coat for 1 side of each door, but 1 litre will be needed to do both sides of each door or more than 1 coat   **d.** 250ml

Dates and Calendars *(p.10)*

1. February 12th   **2.** April 27th   **3.** December 4th   **4.** August 12th
5. December 10th   **6.** Tuesday   **7.** July 2nd   **8.** April 1st

Migraine Tablets *(p.11)*

Adults: 1. False   **2.** True - 2 pink tablets at first, followed by 2 yellow tablets 4 hours later.   **3.** False - not throughout the day. A maximum of 6 yellow tablets in 24 hours.   **4.** True   **5.** False - except if affected by drowsiness.   **6.** True
Children: 1. True   **2.** True   **3.** False   **4.** True, and they shouldn't take pink ones either!

Olympic High Jump *(p.12/13)*

1. **a.** Higher - many door frames are around 2.1 metres
   b. Higher - the ceiling height in a new house is about 2.3 metres
2. 1928
3. **a.** 1936   **b.** 1984
4. **a.** 1992   **b.** 1992
5. 1952 and all previous Games
6. About 0.3 metres (actually 0.28)

Patio *(p.14)*

1. 60 slabs
2. 4 packs
3. £165
4. **a.** 60 slabs (but some will need to be trimmed if the patio cannot be made a little larger)   **b.** £63   **c.** £102

Pub prices *(p.15)*

1. About £10, perhaps.
2. £4.20 (although many pubs charge a little more than half the pint cost)
3. £7.60
4. £6.05
5 **a.** £6.75   **b.** £3.25
6. **a.** No - it would cost £8.40
   b. Buy pints for everyone else and a half for yourself. *Total:* £7.35

Shopping sizes *(p.16/17)*

Eggs   a. 6 *(half a dozen)*   **b.** By the box or by the dozen   **c.** Size 1

Coffee   a. 50g   **b.** Cheapest own brand could be 99p. Well-known brand names can be as much as £1.59. Special coffees *(e.g. Gold Blend Decaffeinated)* can be as much as £2.92.

Butter 250g   **Cheese** £1.65   **Crisps** £10.80

Fruit Juice 1 litre *(family-size carton)* **or** 250ml or 200ml *(small individual carton)*

Bread About 22   **Sardines** £3.08   **Wine** 75cl

Making Custard *(p.18)*

1. 1 to 2 tablespoons (according to sweetness preferred).
2. No   3. No
4. 3 minutes (so that you can take it out and stir it), then 3 minutes more.
5. About 7 minutes.   6. Probably not much.   7. Yes
8. *In practice:* Use half quantities and either eat a bit more or save some for another meal! *In theory (using a calculator):* 0.8 tablespoons custard powder; 0.4 - 0.8 tablespoons sugar; 8 fl. oz. (227ml) milk.

Distances *(p.19)*

4. 60 m.p.h.;   97 k.p.h.

Wallpaper *(p.20)*

1. 12.48 sq. metres   2. 2.4 sq. m.   3. 10.08 sq. m.   4. 5.2 sq. m.
5. In theory, 2 rolls will do it but, in practice, 3 will be needed to allow for cutting pieces to fit round the window and the edges.
6. 3 x £6.49 = £19.47 + the cost of the paste.

Wallpaper paste *(p.21)*

1. 10 rolls   2. 4 or 5   3. 8 pints   4. 1 gallon (8 pints)
5. No - put the water in first and then add contents
6. No - stir briskly, leave for 3 minutes and stir again
7. 160 sq. ft.   8. 640 tiles

TV Guide *(p.22/23)*

1.   a. 30 minutes   b. Half an hour
2.   One and a half hours (90 minutes)
3.   20 minutes
4.   95 minutes
5.   8.00 p.m. (2000 hours)
6.   4.10 a.m. (0410 hours)
7.   1830 and 1900 hours
8.   No - unless you had a video with a long-play facility.
9.   In theory, you might miss the last 5 minutes of 'motorsport' but, in practice, tapes usually last a little longer than stated.
10.   a. 1800 and 1830   b. 2100 and 2200   c. 2330 and 0035

Fractions, decimals and percentages *(p.24/25)*
A.

	1 Fraction	2 Decimal	3 Percentage	4 Proportion
Half	1/2	0.5	50%	1 in 2
Third	1/3	0.33	33.3%	1 in 3
Quarter	1/4	0.25	25%	1 in 4
Fifth	1/5	0.2	20%	1 in 5
Eighth	1/8	0.125	12.5%	1 in 8
Tenth	1/10	0.1	10%	1 in 10

B.
a. 1/3 (33.3%)
b. 1/8 (12.5%)
c. 1/4 (25%)
d. 1/2 (50%)
e. 1/10 (10%)
f. 1/5 (20%)

McDonald's *(p.26/27)*

1. Because McDonald's is American and in the U.S. chips are usually called *French Fries*, while potato crisps are called chips ! *Regular* is a more common word in America and the word *small*, in marketing terms, could also imply meanness.
2. 31p
3. **a.** £1.68 **b.** 32p
4. **a.** £2.79 **b.** £7.21
5. **a.** £1.45 **b.** £3.55
6. **a.** £2.99 **b.** £17.01
7. 26.5p; 24.6p; 22.7p
8. *Suggestion:* One Medium Meal *(£2.99)*, two Children's Happy Meals *(£1.99 each)* and two ice cream cones *(45p each)*. *Total:* £7.87

Cars for Sale *(p.28/29)*

1. 16 *(all the cars are Fords)*
2. Car *n*.
3. Cars *f*. and *p*.
4. Perhaps £4,600 ?
5. Between 1/8/96 and 31/7/97
6. The registration letters began to be changed twice yearly - on 1st September and 1st March, instead of once a year on 1st August.
7. They have the same size engine. 1300cc is the same as 1.3 litres.
8. **a.** Car **i**. *(£1290)*   **b.** Car **h**. *(£11,000)*
9. Probably a *Ford Fiesta* (**b**. and **c**.) or a *Ford Ka* (**j**. and **k**.)
10. *l. to r.* full service history; current Ministry of Transport Test Certificate; part exchange; power assisted steering; anti-lock brake system; electric windows; central locking; 90,000 miles (*K* is short for *kilo*, which means *1,000*, as in <u>*kilo*</u>*gram* or <u>*kilo*</u>*metre*)

Maths about the house - 2 *(p.30/31)*

1. **Plugs and Fuses**
   a. 13 amp   **b.** Small: 3 amp   **c.** Electric cooker

2. **Ironing**

   a.   **b.** Cooler

   c.   **d.**

3. **Cooking maths**
   a. tablespoon
   b. litre *(= 1.76 pints)*
   c. ounce *(= 28.4g)*
   d. kilogram *(= 2.2 lb)*
   e. Gas Mark 8 *(= 230°C or 450°F)*

4. **Paper**
   a. A1   **b.** A4
   c. About 200mm x 300mm *or* 8″ x 12″ *(exact size is 210mm x 297mm)*
   d. A5   **e.** C5

Fridge Freezers *(p.32/33)*
1. *Candy* - £319.99   2. *Zanussi* - £399.99   3. £70   4. £50
5. The *Siemens* appears to be the best bargain because it gives the biggest saving in proportion to the original cost.
6. Manufacturers offer different discounts to the shop, but the bigger reductions could also be because models are less popular or because they have been (or are about to be) replaced by new models.
7. **a.** £210   **b.** £390   **c.** £609.99   **d.** £769.99
   e. The *Zanussi* is the cheaper by £160.
   (**N.B.** *The running costs of these models are true figures from tests by* **Which?** *magazine, November 1999)*

World population *(p.36/37)*
1. **In 1950: a.** Africa   **b.** Asia   **c.** Developed countries   **d.** Latin America   **e.** Two and a half billion
2. **By 2025: a.** Eight and a half billion   **b.** Six billion   **c.** Asia
   d. It will have more than doubled from 9% to 19%
   e. It will have halved from 32% to 16%
3. **Cities of the world: a.** Shanghai   **b.** London   **c.** Cairo, Jakarta, Tehran & Karachi   **d.** Mexico City   **e.** Shanghai & London

Travel in the U.K. *(p.38/39)*
1. By coach - *National Express* Advanced Return, £25.
2. By air - *British Airways,* full price, £286.
3. £261   4. £178   5. Train (or air?)
6. Air + taxi/underground probably, but not a lot quicker than the train.
7. Coach (or car?)   **8.** Car   **9.** Car   **10.** £266

Gas Bill *(p.40)*
1. 403   2. £59.15   3. £65.38 + VAT @ 5% *(£3.27)* = £68.65
4. £15.87

Wood Filler Instructions *(p.41)*
1. c.   2. c.   3. **a.** False   **b.** True   **c.** True   **d.** True (although the instructions don't tell you this).

Index

This index is intended only as a rough guide to the topics and skills covered.
Estimation and the four rules of number occur too frequently to be indexed.